Anna School Learning

MATH WORKBOOK

Step by Step Guide

Name:_____

Class:_____

Teacher:_____

Contents

Order of Operations (PEMDAS)

The order of operations, often remembered by the acronym PEMDAS, stands for:

- **Parentheses**: Perform operations inside parentheses first.
- **Exponents**: Evaluate exponents (powers and roots) next.
- **Multiplication and Division**: Perform multiplication and division from left to right.
- **Addition and Subtraction**: Perform addition and subtraction from left to right.

The order of operations helps to clarify which operations should be performed first in a mathematical expression to ensure consistent and accurate results.

- **Parentheses**: Evaluate expressions within parentheses first. If there are nested parentheses, start with the innermost ones and work your way out.

  1. Example: $2 \times (3 + 4) = 2 \times 7 = 14$

- **Exponents**: Evaluate expressions with exponents (powers and roots) next.

  1. Example: $2^3 + 4 = 8 + 4 = 12$

- **Multiplication and Division**: Perform multiplication and division from left to right.

  1. Example: $2 \times 3 + 4 = 6 + 4 = 10$

  2. Example: $6 \div 2 \times 3 = 3 \times 3 = 9$

- **Addition and Subtraction**: Perform addition and subtraction from left to right.

  1. Example: $2 + 3 \times 4 = 2 + 12 = 14$

  2. Example: $10 - 4 \div 2 = 10 - 2 = 8$

Order of Operations (PEMDAS)

1. $(10 + 10)(10 + 6) =$

2. $(5 + 3)^2 =$

3. $(5 + 3) \times (6 + 3) =$

4. $(5 \times 9) - (3 + 10) =$

5. $9 + 4 - 5 + 8 =$

6. $(7 + 6)(7 + 10) =$

7. $5 \times 3 =$

8. $(8 + 3)^2 =$

9. $4 + 10 + 10 =$

10. $8 \times 9 =$

Anna School Learning

11. $(3 + 4)(2 + 10) =$

12. $8 \times (3 + 5) =$

13. $(7 \times 3) - (6 + 8) =$

14. $(6 \times 8) - (3 + 2) =$

15. $9 \times 3 =$

16. $10 \times 6 + 2 =$

17. $(10 \times 1) - (10 + 10) =$

18. $(4 + 3) \times (2 + 7) =$

19. $2 + 2 - 10 + 10 =$

20. $4 + 5^2 =$

Anna School Learning

21. $(4^2) \times (7^2) + 10 =$

22. $2 \times 6 + 3 =$

23. $7 + 6 + 4 + 9 =$

24. $(5 + 5)^2 =$

25. $(4 + 8)^2 =$

26. $(6 + 8)^2 =$

27. $(6 + 9)(9 + 3) =$

28. $(5 + 8)^2 + (1 + 7)^2 =$

29. $2 + 10^2 =$

30. $(2 + 7) \times (9 + 3) =$

Anna School Learning

31. $10 \times 1 + 6 =$

32. $9(10 + 7) =$

33. $(9 + 3)^2 + (5 + 10)^2 =$

34. $10 \times (1 + 3) =$

35. $3(1 + 7) =$

36. $(1 + 2) \div 7 =$

37. $7 + 8 - 7 + 7 =$

38. $9 + 5^2 =$

39. $5 \times 4 \times 2 =$

40. $(5^2) \times (10^2) + 1 =$

41. $1 \times 7 \times 1 =$

42. $8 \times 5 + 8 =$

43. $\left(7^2\right) \times \left(1^2\right) + 3 =$

44. $3 + 10 + 3 + 8 =$

45. $(3 + 6) \div 9 =$

46. $5 + 6 + 1 + 10 =$

47. $(4 + 6)^2 =$

48. $\left(8^2\right) \times \left(5^2\right) + 10 =$

49. $3 + 6 + 9 =$

50. $10 \times 9 =$

Solving One-Step Equations

Solving one-step equations involves finding the value of the variable that makes the equation true. In a one-step equation, there is only one operation (addition, subtraction, multiplication, or division) performed on the variable.

The goal is to isolate the variable on one side of the equation by performing inverse operations.

For example:

Given the equation 6 = -3z, where we want to solve for z.

The given equation is already in the form of a one-step equation, with z being multiplied by -3.

To isolate z, we need to perform the inverse operation of multiplication, which is division.

Divide both sides by -3:

$$\frac{6}{-3} = \frac{-3z}{-3}$$

Simplify:

$$-2 = z$$

So, the solution to the equation is z = -2.

When we substitute the value of z = -2 back into the original equation, 6 = -3(-2), it simplifies to 6 = 6. This confirms that our solution is correct because it satisfies the original equation.

Solving Two-Step Equations

Solving two-step equations involves finding the value of the variable that makes the equation true. In a two-step equation, two operations (addition, subtraction, multiplication, or division) are performed on the variable.

The goal is to isolate the variable on one side of the equation by performing inverse operations in the reverse order of operations.

For example:

Given the equation $18 = (10 + b) - 2$, where we want to solve for b.

To solve for b, we need to undo the operations that have been performed on b.

1. Undo the subtraction by adding 2 to both sides:

$$18 + 2 = (10 + b) - 2 + 2$$

$$20 = 10 + b$$

2. Undo the addition by subtracting 10 from both sides:

$$20 - 10 = 10 + b - 10$$

$$10 = b$$

So, the solution to the equation is $b = 10$

Let's substitute $b = 10$ back into the original equation to verify if it satisfies the equation:

Original equation:

$$18 = (10 + b) - 2:$$

Substitute $b = 10$:

$$18 = (10 + 10) - 2$$

simplify:

$$18 = 20 - 2$$

$$18 = 18$$

Since the equation simplifies to 18 =1 8, it confirms that our solution $b = 10$ is correct.

Solving Multi-Step Equations

Solving multi-step equations involves finding the value of the variable that makes the equation true. In a multi-step equation, multiple operations (addition, subtraction, multiplication, or division) are performed on the variable.

The goal is to isolate the variable on one side of the equation by performing inverse operations in the reverse order of operations.

Example:

Given the equation $-3m - m = -8$, where we want to solve for m.

To solve for m, we need to undo the operations that have been performed on m.

1. Combine like terms on the left side:

$$-3m - m = -4m$$

2. Substitute the combined term back into the equation:

$$-4m = -8$$

3. Undo the multiplication by dividing both sides by -4-4:

$$\frac{-4m}{-4} = \frac{-8}{-4}$$

$$m = 2$$

Let's substitute m = 2 back into the original equation to verify if it satisfies the equation:

Original equation:

$$-3m - m = -8$$

Substitute m = 2:

$$-3(2) - 2 = -8$$

simplify:

$$-6 - 2 = -8$$

$$-8 = -8$$

Since the equation simplifies to 8 = 8, it confirms that our solution m = 2 is correct.

One-Step Equations
Solve for the variable.

1. $8(2 - z) = -8$

2. $10 + (m \div 9) = 10.9$

3. $2 + (3 \cdot k) = 17$

4. $a \cdot 5 = 50$

5. $7y - y = 48$

6. $4 = (y \cdot 3) + y$

7. $9 \cdot x + x = 80$

8. $15 = 4s - s$

9. $54 = 5 \cdot s + s$

10. $3x + x = 36$

11. $2 \cdot (x - 3) = 8$

12. $72 = 10m - m$

13. $10 + (y \div 4) = 11.5$

14. $(9 \cdot x) + 7 = 88$

15. $1 = s \div 1$

16. $m \cdot (5 - m) = -6$

17. $a \cdot (6 - a) = -40$

18. $9 + (10 \cdot k) = 39$

19. $6 \div y = 6$

20. $-18 = y \cdot (7 - y)$

21. $y \cdot (9 - y) = 0$

22. $0.9 = a \div 9$

23. $3 + (3 \cdot m) = 30$

24. $34 = 10 + 6z$

25. $m \cdot (8 - m) = 16$

26. $8 \cdot (b - 1) = 0$

27. $8 + m = 16$

28. $3 \cdot b = 15$

29. $a \cdot 4 = 12$

30. $10 = a + (9 \div a)$

Anna School Learning

31. $11 = 10 + (m \div 8)$

32. $11 = 10 + b$

33. $66 = 10s + s$

34. $9 \div b = 9$

35. $(x \div 6) + x = 9.3$

36. $-2 = 4 + (s - 9)$

37. $34 = s \cdot 4 + 10$

38. $(m \cdot 8) + m = 45$

39. $9.9 = (8 \div b) + 9$

40. $x + (6 \div x) = 9.7$

41. $m + (m \cdot 9) = 40$

42. $9 + (z - 1) = 16$

43. $9b + 10 = 19$

44. $35 = 5(1 + m)$

45. $77 = y \cdot 8 + 5$

46. $35 = x \cdot 4 + x$

47. $9 = m \cdot 8 + m$

48. $42 = 7(5 + a)$

49. $0.8 = k \div 10$

50. $12 = 1 \cdot x + x$

Two-Step Equations

Solve for the variable.

1. $(3 + x) \cdot 6 = 24$

2. $(4z)^2 = 64$

3. $1 = (7 - x) \cdot 1$

4. $8 + (z + 6) = 19$

5. $6 \cdot (1 + x) = 60$

6. $2z + 2 = 4$

7. $7 = 5 + (1 \cdot x)$

8. $(y)^2 = 1$

9. $2 = (3 - x) \cdot 2$

10. $(6 \cdot y) + 3 = 21$

11. $48 = 7y + 5y$

12. $3x + 7x = 10$

13. $(3y)^2 = 144$

14. $-6 = (6 - z) \cdot 6$

15. $8 \cdot x + 8 = 32$

16. $27 = 9 \cdot (2 + y)$

17. $44 = 2z + 3 + (4z - 1)$

18. $-5 = 3z + z - 9$

19. $12 = z^2 + z - 8$

20. $(7 \cdot z) - 5 = 44$

Anna School Learning

21. $z + 7 + 5z = 37$

22. $8 = z + 6z - 6$

23. $27 = (2 \cdot x) + 9$

24. $17 = 7 + (2 \cdot y)$

25. $z(7 + z) = 60$

26. $y + 2y - 6 = 9$

27. $(5 - x) \cdot 4 = -12$

28. $3 = x + 2$

29. $y(9 + y) = 112$

30. $576 = (3z)^2$

Multi-Step Equations

Solve for the variable.

1. $9z + 7 \cdot (z + 7) - 7 = 58$

2. $(z + 1) + (7z + 2) = 43$

3. $282 = 9 + (4x - x)(6 + x)$

4. $4(x - 5) + 6x = 70$

5. $(4y + 2) \cdot (y + 3) = 24$

6. $(5y + 9) + (2y - 6) = 17$

7. $810 = 4x^2 + 6x^2$

8. $(3 \cdot z) + 5z - 4 = 4$

Anna School Learning

9. $7(y + 4) + y(8 - y) = 42$

10. $-10 = 2 + (x - 5)(2x)$

11. $36 = 6(z + 2) + (9z - 6)$

12. $2y^2 + 4y^2 = 150$

13. $(5z + 7) \cdot (z - 2) = 54$

14. $3(z + 7) + z = 41$

15. $6y + 8(y + 5) - y = 66$

16. $6x + 3(x + 5) - x = 63$

17. $648 = (7z + 8)(6z - 6)$

18. $17 = (9y + 1) + (5y + 2)$

19. $-1 = 5(2x - 7) + 3(7 + x)$

20. $(3x + 3) \cdot (x + 7) = 120$

21. $(8y + 5)(3y + 7) = 990$

22. $60 = (2x + 6) + (5x - 9)$

23. $-53 = 1 + z(2 - z) + z$

24. $2y + (9 \cdot y) - 1 = 32$

Solving Equations (One Side)

Solving one-step equations involves performing a single operation to isolate the variable and find its value.

Let's solve an equation step by step: 16 + x = 31

1. **Identify the Goal:**

    The goal is to isolate the variable x on one side of the equation.

2. **Simplify the Equation:** Combine like terms on both sides of the equation, if necessary.

    The equation is already simplified.

3. **Undo Addition or Subtraction:** If there's addition or subtraction involving the variable, undo it by performing the opposite operation on both sides of the equation.

    Since x is being added to 16, we'll undo this operation by subtracting 16 from both sides of the equation:
    $$16 + x - 16 = 31 - 16$$

4. **Isolate the Variable:** Ensure that the variable is alone on one side of the equation.

    $$X = 15$$

5. **Check Your Solution:** Substitute the value of x back into the original equation to verify that it satisfies the equation.

    $$16 + 15 = 31$$

    $$31 = 31$$

The equation is balanced, so the solution.

Equations: (One Side)

Solve the equations for the variable.

1. $3k - -9 = 12$

2. $x + -10 = -2$

3. $8z + 3 = -77$

4. $1x - 4 = 1$

5. $k \times 19 = -114$

6. $17 \times z = 306$

7. $-8 + 8x = 16$

8. $-6y + -10 = -46$

9. $9k + 3 = -78$

10. $-9 \times m = 45$

11. $x + 9 = 0$

12. $-1k + 8 = 14$

13. $3z - -8 = 62$

14. $-5z + 20 = 30$

15. $9 + k = 20$

16. $3 \times z = 9$

17. $-84 \div x = -7$

18. $k - 8 = 9$

19. $z \div 14 = 1$

20. $2 + 1x = 7$

Anna School Learning

21. $1y - 3 = 1$

22. $27 - 3y = 3$

23. $k \times 3 = 39$

24. $14 \times y = 238$

25. $5y - 17 = 3$

26. $5y - 20 = 0$

27. $6 \times k = -48$

28. $1k - 6 = 12$

29. $10 \div x = 5$

30. $x - -8 = 17$

31. $m + -2 = -5$

32. $-9x + -10 = 71$

33. $3 \times z = 57$

34. $y - 17 = 0$

35. $m \times 7 = 140$

36. $17 \times k = 340$

37. $96 \div k = 6$

38. $k \div -7 = -8$

39. $6 - y = 7$

40. $17 - 8y = 1$

41. $13 + 6m = 73$

42. $k + -7 = 1$

43. $14 - 1z = 2$

44. $x - -3 = 23$

45. $x \div -2 = 16$

46. $y \times -7 = -14$

47. $k \div 14 = 6$

48. $m \div 12 = 19$

49. $9 + m = 4$

50. $20 \times k = -160$

51. $12 \times k = -60$

52. $-4 + 6m = -34$

53. $30 \div m = 3$

54. $y + 14 = 33$

55. $12 - y = 13$

56. $15 - 0x = 15$

57. $4 \times y = -12$

58. $k \times 15 = 300$

59. $z - -8 = 17$

60. $-9z + -4 = -4$

Equations (Two Sides)

A two-sided equation is an equation where both sides have expressions with variables and constants. The goal when solving a two-sided equation is to find the value of the variable that makes both sides equal.

For example: Let's solve an equation:

$$9 + 8x + 8 = 64 + x + 2$$

- **Combine Like Terms:** Simplify each side of the equation by combining like terms (terms with the same variable or constants).

$$9 + 8x + 8 = 64 + x + 2$$
$$17 + 8x = 66 + x$$

- **Isolate the Variable:** Use inverse operations to isolate the variable on one side of the equation.

subtract x from both sides:

$$17 + 8x - x = 66 + x - x$$

$$17 + 7x = 66$$

subtracting 17 from both sides:

$$17 - 17 + 7x = 66 - 17$$

$$7x = 49$$

divide both sides by 7:

$$\frac{7x}{7} = \frac{49}{7} = x = 7$$

- **Check Solution:** Once you find the solution, substitute it back into the original equation to ensure it makes the equation true.

Substitute $x = 7$ back into the original equation:

$$9 + 8(7) + 8 = 64 + 7 + 2$$

$$9 + 56 + 8 = 64 + 7 + 2$$

$$73 = 73$$

Equations (Two Sides)

Solve for the variable.

1. $-6x = -15 - x$

2. $34 - y + 13 = -8 + 6y + 6$

3. $67 - y + -3 = 4 + -7y + 6$

4. $30 + b = -9b$

5. $-9 + 7b = 31 - b$

6. $-3 + 4s = 3 + s$

7. $-1 + 2s = -22 - s$

8. $3 + -7a + 2 = -11 + a$

9. $-6z = 56 + z$

10. $-2a + -1 = -8 + 5a$

11. $6 + -10x = 17 + x$

12. $1 + -6x = 31 - x$

13. $7 - a = -2a + 8$

14. $9x = -72 + x$

15. $8 + 2x = 4x + -4$

16. $-4 - a = -3a$

17. $28 + x = 8x$

18. $6 + 4z = -39 - z$

19. $-6k + 3 = -37 - k$

20. $-17 + b = -9 + 5b$

21. $2m = -21 - m$

22. $-90 - z = -10z$

23. $-6 - z = -2z$

24. $-53 + -10s = 1 + 8s$

25. $-5 + 10a = -39 - 7a$

26. $-48 + a = -7a$

27. $-13 - -7y = 9y + 7$

28. $-2m = 15 + m$

29. $15 + b + 13 = 3 + -4b + 10$

30. $-3x = -4 - x$

31. $-2 + -4k = -17 - k$

32. $-6 + 2m + -6 = -24 + m + 3$

33. $-22 + z = -3z + 6$

34. $3b + 6 = 18 - b$

35. $7y + -5 = -1 + 8y$

36. $-33 - b + -6 = -6 + -9b + -9$

37. $-10 - b = 4b$

38. $-41 + y = 9y + 7$

39. $-13 - -10a = 7a + -10$

40. $4 + 5s = 13 - 4s$

41. $9x + -9 = 91 - x$

42. $56 + m + 16 = 2 + -9m + 10$

43. $-3 + 6b + -1 = -74 - b$

44. $-9 + 3k + -8 = -41 - k$

45. $58 + b = 4 + -8b$

46. $-4 + x = 9 + -10x + 9$

47. $2 + 4m = -3m + 58$

48. $2m = -30 - m$

49. $44 + k = -10k$

50. $5 + 3a = -3a + -1$

Simplifying Expressions

It involves combining like terms and performing operations to make the expression easier to understand and work with.

Let's simplify the expression:

$$2x - 2x + 8 + 4$$

- **Combine like terms:** First, we look for terms with the same variable and exponent. In this expression, $2x$ and $-2x$ are like terms, so they can be combined:

$$2x - 2x = 0$$

- **Substitute the simplified terms:** After combining the like terms, the expression becomes:

$$0 + 8 + 4$$

- **Combine the remaining terms:** Now, we add the constants together

$$: 8 + 4 = 12$$

Date: _____/_____/_____

Simplify Expressions

1. $11k + 18 - 4 - 4k + 6k$

2. $4 + 13k - 13k + 7 - 8k$

3. $y - 4y$

4. $-z + 14 + 9z$

5. $-15 + 18z + 18 - 11z$

6. $10m - m$

7. $-16y + y$

8. $-17 - 10k + 2k - 4 + 2k$

9. $-8k - 12k$

10. $-16 - 17m + 12m - 5 + 7m$

Anna School Learning

11. $-2x - 8 + 11x$

12. $12 + k - 11 + 14k$

13. $20m - 20m + 16 + 13$

14. $x + 15 + 19x$

15. $-18y - 18 + 15y$

16. $x + 3 + 7x$

17. $16 - 19k + 3 - 5k + 18 - k$

18. $5 + 17m - 17 + 7m$

19. $18 + 6(18k - 3)$

20. $-5m - 8m$

Date: ____/____/_____

21. $-15z + z$

22. $14 + 17x - x$

23. $12k - 18 - 8k + 7$

24. $-2z - 13 - 2z$

25. $-11k + 5k$

26. $19k - 19 - 20k + 2 - 8$

27. $12z - 7 - 12z + 10$

28. $-x + 15x$

29. $-m + 13m$

30. $3m + 7 + m$

Anna School Learning

31. $5m + m$

32. $-15 - 13x + 8 - 3x$

33. $z + 10z$

34. $-2x - 13 + 15x$

35. $18z - 8 - 19z + 3$

36. $x - 3x + 4x + 12 + 3$

37. $-z - 8z$

38. $-16 - 15k + 12k - 8 + 17k$

39. $-16 + 5k + 17 - 7k$

40. $-13 + 2 - x + 4x - 4 + 14x$

Date: _____/_____/_____

41. $-15 - 12y + 5y - 14 + 11y$

42. $-9y - 13y$

43. $-17z - 14 - 7z$

44. $-6m - 17 - 5m$

45. $16y - 12 + 18y - 7 + 7y + 11$

46. $-19x + 10 + 5x + 1 + 4x - 1$

47. $-5z - 6 + 5z$

48. $-18m + 14 - 19m$

49. $k - 5k + 15 + 12$

50. $15x - 17 - 18x + 14$

51. $3m - 14 - 9m + 7$

52. $-13x - 10 - 6 - 14x$

53. $13 + m - 5 + 15m$

54. $-11y + y$

55. $-14z + 15 - 16 + 12z$

56. $13y + 9 - 8 - 11y + 19y$

57. $10y + 9 + 12y + 20 + 18y + 9$

58. $11y + 2y$

59. $-10x + 9x + 2 - 3x$

60. $-19z + 15z$

Evaluate Expressions

Evaluating expressions involves substituting given values for variables in an expression and then performing the indicated operations to find the result.

For example: Let's evaluate 4x – 10, when x = 3:

Step 1: Substitute the given value for the variable:

Replace every occurrence of x in the expression 4x – 10 with the given value, which is 3:

$$= 4(3) - 10$$

Step 2: Perform the operations:

Perform the indicated operations according to the order of operations (PEMDAS - Parentheses, Exponents, Multiplication and Division, Addition and Subtraction):

$$= 4 \times 3 - 10$$

Step 3: Simplify:

Calculate the result:

$$12 - 10 = 2$$

Evaluating Equations

Simplify the following equations when the value of $n = -5$

1. $-10 + (8n + 5) - -4 + (-2n) =$

2. $-6(n + 4) + 5n =$

3. $(-2 + n)(-7n - 8) =$

4. $n + 6 =$

5. $-3 + (n - -1) =$

6. $8 + (n \div -10) =$

7. $-5n - -7 + -10n =$

8. $n \cdot 7 + -9 =$

Anna School Learning

Evaluating Equations

Simplify the following equations when the value of n = –5

1. $(-2 + n)(-8n - 9) =$

2. $(-7n + -7)(10n - 8) =$

3. $2 + (n - 6)(8n) =$

4. $(n \cdot 9) + n =$

5. $-2 + (n - 7)(8n) =$

6. $-5 \cdot n + -5 =$

7. $-9n + 10 \cdot (n + -6) =$

8. $-8 \div n =$

Evaluating Equations

Simplify the following equations when the value of n = -4

1. -5(0 + n) + -3n – 6 =

2. -7 + 0n =

3. 5n + n =

4. -6n + 10(n – -9) =

5. 2n – 4 + -3n =

6. -10n + 4(n + 8) – n =

7. 10 + (-2n – n)(6 + n) =

8. -1 • n – -2 =

Evaluating Equations

Simplify the following equations when the value of $n = 2$

1. $n \cdot -6 + 5 =$

2. $3 \cdot n + 1 =$

3. $-2n^2 + 0n^3 =$

4. $3 \cdot n + n =$

5. $-5 \cdot n + 0 =$

6. $-6n - -3 + -3n =$

7. $0n + 9 \cdot (n - 6) =$

8. $(-1 \div n) + -3 =$

Evaluating Equations

Simplify the following equations when the value of $n = -5$

1. $8n + n =$

2. $4 \cdot n + -7 =$

3. $10n + -3 \cdot (n - 4) =$

4. $n + -5 \cdot (n + -4) - 4 =$

5. $n \cdot 4 - 1 =$

6. $(3 - n) \cdot (6n + 9) =$

7. $3(4 + n) + 6n - -6 =$

8. $-6(-4 + n) + -3n - 5 =$

Anna School Learning

Evaluating Equations

Simplify the following equations when the value of $n = -4$

1. $-10(0n - -1) + -1(7 + n) =$

2. $0 \cdot (-3 + n) =$

3. $7 + (n \div -8) =$

4. $(-4n)^1 =$

5. $-5 + (9n + -10) =$

6. $2n + -3 \cdot (n + 9) =$

7. $-6n + -4 \cdot (n + -8) - 2 =$

8. $10 + -8n =$

Find Numbers (Verbal Algebra)

Verbal algebra involves translating word problems or verbal statements into algebraic expressions or equations.

For example: The product of the two numbers is 91. One number is six less than the other. What are the numbers?

We're given a verbal description of a problem, and we need to represent it using algebraic symbols and equations.

Let's break down the given problem into algebraic expressions:

- Given that the product of the two numbers is 91, we can write the equation: $xy = 91$
- Also, given that one number is six less than the other, we can write another equation: $x = y - 6$

Now, we can use algebraic techniques to solve the system of equations to find the values of x and y, which represent the two numbers.

$$x(x - 6) = 91$$

1. Solve the equation:

   - Expand the equation:

   $$x^2 - 6x = 91$$

   - Rearrange the equation into standard quadratic form:

   $$x^2 - 6x - 91 = 0$$

   - Factor the quadratic equation:

   $$(x - 13)(x + 7) = 0$$

2. Find the solutions for x:

   - From the factored form, we have two possible values for x:

   $$x = 13 \text{ or } x = -7$$

3. **Check the validity of the solutions:**

- Since one number is six less than the other, we discard the negative solution.

- Therefore, the solution is $x = 13$.

4. **Find the other number:**

- Substitute $x = 13$ into the expression for the other number:

Other number $= x - 6 = 13 - 6 = 7$

So, the two numbers are 13 and 7.

Verbal Algebra

1. One number is eight times another. Their sum is 54. Find the numbers.

2. Two-thirds of a number increased by 2 is 8. What is the number?

3. Five times a number equals 32 less than nine times the number. What is the number?

4. If the product of seven and a number is increased by 4, the result is 67. Find the number?

5. One of two numbers is seven more than the other. The sum of the numbers is 11. Find the numbers.

6. A number diminished by 3 is 5. Find the number.

7.   One less than seven times a number is 83. Find the number.

8.   One number is nine times another. Their sum is 50. Find the numbers.

9.   Four-fifths of a number decreased by 1 is 7. Find the number.

10.   Three times a number is 6. What is the number?

11.   One of two numbers is two-fifths of the other number. The sum of the numbers is 7. Find the numbers.

12.   A number increased by two is 7. Find the number.

13. One of two numbers is one-third of the other number. The sum of the numbers is 4. Find the numbers.

14. Four times the difference of 13 minus a number is 12. What is the number?

15. Eight times a number increased by 8 is 56. Find the number.

16. One number is ten times another. Their sum is 44. Find the numbers.

17. One of two numbers is four more than the other. The sum of the numbers is 20. Find the numbers.

18. One of two numbers is three more than the other. The sum of the numbers is 9. Find the numbers.

Anna School Learning

19. The sum of a number and seven is 15. Find the number.

20. The sum of three consecutive odd numbers is 27. Find the numbers.

21. Six times a number is 0. What is the number?

22. The sum of four consecutive even numbers is 44. What are the numbers?

23. Eight more than four times a number is equal to the number increased by 35. What is the number?

24. A number diminished by 5 is 9. Find the number.

Anna School Learning

25. Twice a number increased by 3 is 7. Find the number.

26. The product of three and a number is 9. What is the number?

27. The sum of two numbers is 10. One number is eight less than the other. Find the numbers.

28. The product of two numbers is 72. One number is six less than the other. What are the numbers?

29. Four times the sum of a number and two times the number is 72. Find the number.

30. One number is ten more than another number. The sum of the larger number and twice the smaller number is 13. Find the numbers?

Linear Equation

A linear equation is an algebraic equation that represents a straight line when graphed on a coordinate plane. It consists of variables raised to the power of 1 (i.e., no exponents higher than 1) and constant coefficients.

The general form of a linear equation in one variable x is:

$$ax + b = 0$$

Where a and b are constants, and x is the variable.

Let's solve the linear equation:

$$-2x + 9 = 5$$

- **Isolate the variable term:** We want to isolate the term containing x on one side of the equation. To do this, we'll move the constant term to the other side. Subtract 9 from both sides:

$$-2x + 9 - 9 = 5 - 9$$

$$-2x = -4$$

- **Divide by the coefficient of the variable:** To solve for x, divide both sides by the coefficient of x, which is -2:

$$\frac{-2x}{-2} = \frac{-4}{-2}$$

$$x = 2$$

Linear Equations

Solve for the variable.

1. $-6x + -5x = -110$

2. $2x + 1 = 1$

3. $4x + -8 = 16$

4. $4(-6x - 5) = -116$

5. $-8y - 0 = 72$

6. $-1y + 9y - 9 = 63$

7. $10y - 0 = 30$

8. $4y + -8y - 10 = -22$

9. $-5x - -7 = -38$

10. $4(-6y - 5) = -92$

Anna School Learning

11. $6y + -1y = 20$

12. $x + -10x - -5 = -4$

13. $5y - 2 = 3$

14. $-2x + -9x - 0 = -11$

15. $-5y = -15$

16. $8x + -9 = -73$

17. $-7x - 2 = 54$

18. $-1(2x - -3) = -21$

19. $y + 8y = -18$

20. $9y + 10 = 100$

Anna School Learning

21. $-9x + -3 = 87$

22. $-2y - 8 = 12$

23. $-2y + 3 = -13$

24. $-5x + 8x = -24$

25. $-4x + -9 = 23$

26. $0x + -4x = 40$

27. $-4(2x - -1) = 52$

28. $3x + -6x = 21$

29. $8x + -7x - 0 = 3$

30. $8x + 2x - 3 = 77$

Slope from Two Points

The slope between two points on a Cartesian coordinate system is a measure of the steepness of the line connecting those points. It's calculated by finding the change in the y-coordinates divided by the change in the x-coordinates.

- The coordinates of the first point as $(x_1, y_1) = (2, -30)$.

- The coordinates of the second point as $(x_2, y_2) = (-5, 40)$.

The formula to calculate the slope (m) between two points:

$$\frac{y_2 - y_1}{x_2 - x_1}$$

$$= \frac{40 - (-30)}{-5 - 2} = \frac{70}{-7}$$

$$\text{Slope} = -10$$

Find Slope from two Points

1. (6, -9) and (3 , -18)

2. (10, 16) and (-6 , 14)

3. (20, 14) and (16 , -8)

4. (19, 19) and (-12 , 1)

5. (-3, -8) and (11 , 13)

6. (-10, 18) and (-16 , 19)

7. (-10, 20) and (8 , -4)

8. (4, 20) and (-14 , 18)

9. (12, -11) and (7 , 20)

10. (-15, -11) and (-17 , 8)

11. (-18, -17) and (-2 , 1)   12. (-19, 12) and (-14 , 16)

13. (5, 13) and (16 , -1)   14. (7, -4) and (4 , 3)

15. (-16, 8) and (-11 , -13)   16. (-17, 4) and (5 , 17)

17. (14, 1) and (-1 , 9)   18. (-13, -18) and (-17 , -20)

19. (-6, -6) and (14 , -4)   20. (3, -16) and (5 , 1)

Anna School Learning

Graphing Linear Equation

Graphing a linear equation involves plotting the points that satisfy the equation on a coordinate plane and connecting them to form a straight line. Linear equations are equations of the form $y = mx + b$, where m represents the slope of the line, and b represents the y-intercept, the point where the line intersects the y-axis.

To graph a linear equation:

1. Identify the slope (m) and y-intercept (b) from the equation.

2. Plot the y-intercept $(0,b))$ as a point on the y-axis.

3. Use the slope to find additional points on the line. The slope represents the change in y for every unit change in x.

4. Connect the points to form a straight line.

For example, to graph the equation:

$$y = \frac{9}{4}x - 8$$

1. **Identify the slope and y-intercept:** The slope is $\frac{9}{4}$, and the y-intercept is -8.

2. **Plot the y-intercept:** Plot the point $(0,-8)$.

3. **Use the slope to plot additional points:** the slop is $\frac{9}{4}$ to find another point. we will move up 9 units and 4 units to the right from the y-intercept to find another point.

4. **Draw the line:** Once we have at least two points, we can draw a straight line.

We can continue this process to plot more points and extend the line further if needed.

$y = \frac{9}{4}x - 8$

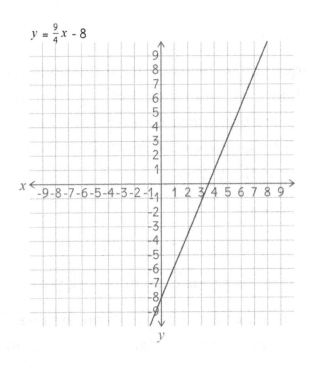

Graphing Linear Equations

1.
$$y = \frac{-3}{2}x + 3$$

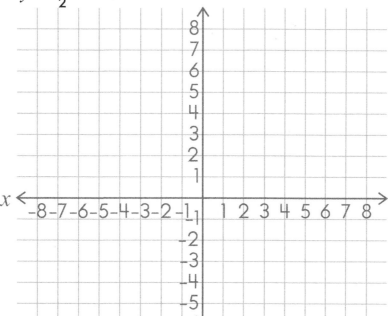

2. $y = \dfrac{-3}{4}x - 7$

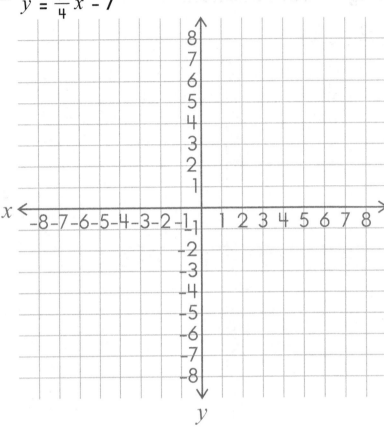

3. $y = -3x - 6$

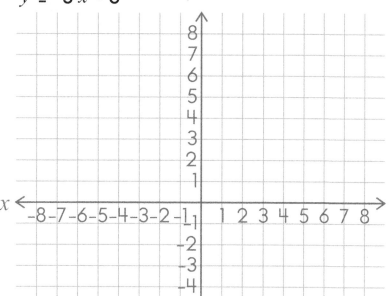

Anna School Learning

4. $y = \dfrac{3}{4}x - 5$

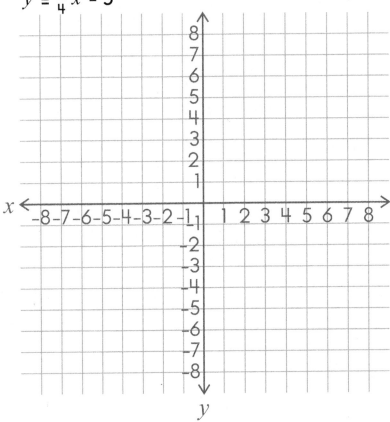

5. $y = 3x$

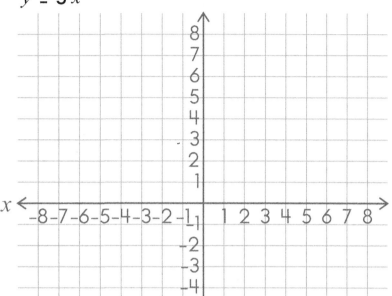

Anna School Learning

Quadratic Equations

A quadratic equation is a polynomial equation of the second degree, meaning it can be written in the form:

$$ax^2 + bx + c = 0$$

where a, b, and c are constants, and x is the variable being solved for. The solutions to a quadratic equation are the values of x that make the equation true.

Now, let's solve the quadratic equation $11x^2 - 1 = 0$ and understand it step by step using quadratic formula.

1. Identify the coefficients:

   In the equation $11x^2 - 1 = 0$,

   $$a=11, b=0, \text{ and } c=-1.$$

2. Apply the quadratic formula:

   The quadratic formula states that for an equation $ax^2 + bx + c = 0$, the solutions for x are given by:

   $$x = \frac{-b \pm \sqrt{b^2 - 4ac}}{2a}$$

   Plugging in the values a=11, b=0, and c=-1 into the quadratic formula, we get:

   $$x = \frac{-0 \pm \sqrt{0 - 4(11)(-1)}}{2(11)}$$

3. Simplify inside the square root:

$$0^2 - 4(11)\,(-1) = 0 - (-44) = 44$$

4. Plug in the simplified values:

$$x = \frac{\pm\sqrt{44}}{22}$$

5. Simplify the square root:

Since 44 is not a perfect square, we can write it as $\sqrt[2]{11}$

$$x = \frac{\pm\sqrt[2]{11}}{22}$$

6. Simplify further if possible:

We can simplify $\sqrt[2]{11}$ to $\sqrt{11}$ by canceling out the common factor:

$$x = \frac{\pm\sqrt{11}}{11}$$

7. Final solution:

So, the solutions to the equation are:

$$x = \frac{\sqrt{11}}{11} \text{ and } x = \frac{-\sqrt{11}}{11}$$

or

$$(x = 0.302, \text{ and } x = -0.302)$$

These are the roots of the quadratic equation. They represent the points where the graph of the quadratic equation intersects the x-axis.

Let's solve another equation:

$$-4p^2 + 6p - 6 = 0$$

$$p = \frac{-b \pm \sqrt{b^2 - 4ac}}{2a}$$

where $a = -4$, $b = 6$, and $c = -6$.

Let's plug these values into the quadratic formula:

$$p = \frac{-6 \pm \sqrt{6^2 - 4(-4)(-6)}}{2(-4)}$$

First, let's simplify inside the square root:

$$6^2 - 4(-4)(-6)$$

$$= 36 - 96 = -60$$

So, we have:

$$p = \frac{-6 \pm \sqrt{-60}}{-8}$$

We can simplify the square root of -60 by factoring out -1:

$$\sqrt{-60}$$

$$= \sqrt{-1 \times 60}$$

$$= \sqrt{-1} \times \sqrt{60}$$

$$= i\sqrt{60}$$

So, we have:

$$p = \frac{-6 \pm i\sqrt{60}}{-8}$$

Simplify:

$$\sqrt{60} \text{ to } \sqrt{4 \times 15} = 2\sqrt{15}$$

$$p = \frac{-6 \pm i \times 2\sqrt{15}}{-8}$$

Now, divide both the numerator and denominator by -2 to simplify:

$$p = \frac{3 \pm i\sqrt{15}}{4}$$

So, the solutions to the equation are:

$$p = \frac{3 + i\sqrt{15}}{4} \text{ and } p = \frac{3 - i\sqrt{15}}{4}$$

This equation $-4p^2 + 6p - 6 = 0$ has no real solutions.

When a quadratic equation has no real solutions, it means that the solutions are not real numbers, but rather complex numbers. In this case, the solutions involve the imaginary unit i because the discriminant ($b^2 - 4ac$) is negative, which results in taking the square root of a negative number when applying the quadratic formula.

In mathematics, such equations are said to have "no real roots" or "no real solutions." They are also sometimes referred to as having "complex roots" or "complex solutions." Complex numbers include a real part and an imaginary part, and they are often written in the form $a + bi$, where a and b are real numbers and i is the imaginary unit, defined as $i = \sqrt{-1}$.

Let's solve another equation:

$$12x^2 + 6x - 2 = 0$$

$$x = \frac{-b \pm \sqrt{b^2 - 4ac}}{2a}$$

where $a = 12$, $b = 6$, and $c = -2$.

Let's plug these values into the quadratic formula:

$$x = \frac{-6 \pm \sqrt{6^2 - 4(12)(-2)}}{2(12)}$$

First, let's simplify inside the square root:

$$6^2 - 4(12)(-2)$$

$$= 36 - (-96)$$

$$= 36 + 96$$

$$= 132$$

So, we have:

$$x = \frac{-6 \pm \sqrt{132}}{24}$$

Now, let's simplify the square root of 132:

$$x = \frac{-6 \pm \sqrt{4 \times 33}}{24}$$

$$x = \frac{-6 \pm 2\sqrt{33}}{24}$$

$$x = \frac{-6 \pm \sqrt{33}}{12}$$

So, the solutions to the equation are:

$$x = \frac{-6 + \sqrt{33}}{12} \text{ and } x = \frac{-6 - \sqrt{33}}{12}$$

$$\text{or } (x = 0.229, \text{ and } x = -0.729)$$

Let's solve a quadratic equation where the right side is a number, instead of 0.

$$-8n^2 + 6n + 30 = 7$$

To solve the equation, we first need to bring all terms to one side to set the equation equal to zero:

$$-8n^2 + 6n + 30 - 7 = 0$$

Simplify:

$$-8n^2 + 6n + 23 = 0$$

Now, to solve for n, we can use the quadratic formula:

$$n = \frac{-b \pm \sqrt{b^2 - 4ac}}{2a}$$

where a = -8, b = 6, and c = 23.

Plugging these values into the formula, we get:

$$n = \frac{-6 \pm \sqrt{6^2 - 4(-8)(23)}}{2(-8)}$$

$$n = \frac{-6 \pm \sqrt{36 + 736}}{-16}$$

$$n = \frac{-6 \pm \sqrt{772}}{-16}$$

Now, let's simplify the square root of 772. We can factor out 4:

$$\sqrt{772} = \sqrt{4 \times 193} = 2\sqrt{193}$$

So, our equation becomes:

$$n = \frac{-6 \pm 2\sqrt{193}}{-8}$$

So, the solutions to the equation are:

$$n = \frac{-3 + \sqrt{193}}{-8} \text{ and } n = \frac{-3 - \sqrt{193}}{-8}$$

or

$$(n = -1.362, \text{ and } n = 2.112)$$

Quadratic Equations

1. $8m^2 + 10m - 24 = 0$

2. $9x^2 - 11 = 0$

3. $x^2 + 6 = 0$

4. $2n^2 - 3n - 104 = 0$

5. $-n^2 + 7n + 4 = 0$

6. $4m^2 - 2m - 72 = 0$

7. $-5n^2 - 4n + 11 = 0$ 10. $4m^2 - m - 9 = -11$

8. $3n^2 + n - 3 = 0$ 11. $-5a^2 + 6a + 60 = -3$

9. $-7p^2 + 12p + 6 = -9$ 12. $n^2 + 4n + 7 = 4$

13. $4m^2 - 5 = 11$

16. $-2a^2 - 3a + 122 = 3$

14. $4n^2 - 113 = 8$

17. $-2a^2 = -10a - 23$

15. $r^2 - 8r - 5 = 10$

18. $-2n^2 - 11n = -51$

19. $12v^2 - 11 = 3v$

22. $5v^2 + 4v = 15$

20. $2v^2 - 22 = 5v$

23. $5k^2 = 6 - 7k$

21. $-6n^2 + 128 = 8n$

24. $x^2 + 8x = -12$

Pythagorean Theorem

The Pythagorean Theorem is a fundamental principle in geometry that relates the lengths of the sides of a right triangle. It states that in any right triangle, the square of the length of the hypotenuse (the side opposite the right angle) is equal to the sum of the squares of the lengths of the other two sides.

$$a2 + b2 = c2$$

Let's use the Pythagorean Theorem to find the length of the hypotenuse (c) when a=44 and b=78.

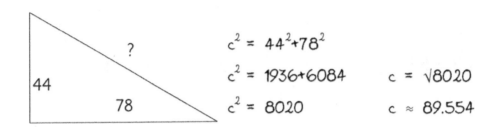

$$c^2 = 44^2 + 78^2$$
$$c^2 = 1936 + 6084$$
$$c^2 = 8020$$

$$c = \sqrt{8020}$$
$$c \approx 89.554$$

Pythagorean Theorem
Find the length of the side.

1.

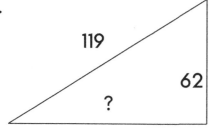

119

62

?

_____

2.

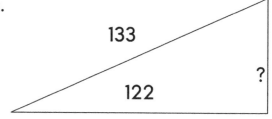

133

122

?

_____

3.

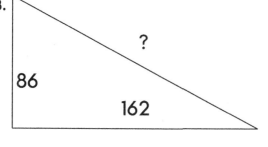

?

86

162

_____

4.

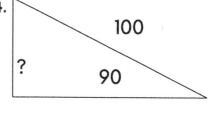

100

?

90

_____

Anna School Learning

5.

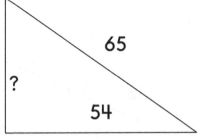

65

?

54

_____

6.

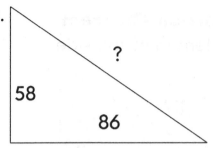

?

58

86

_____

7.

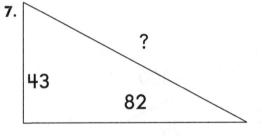

?

43

82

_____

8.

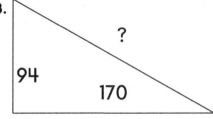

?

94

170

_____

9.

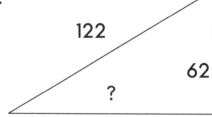

122

62

?

_____

10.

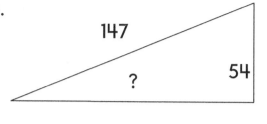

147

54

?

_____

11.

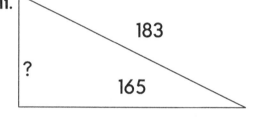

183

?

165

_____

12.

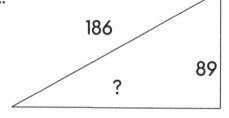

186

89

?

_____

13.

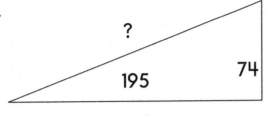

14.

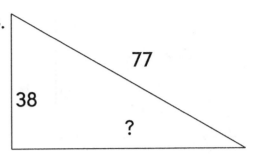

15.

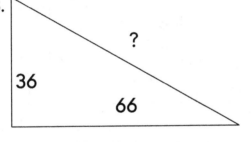

16.

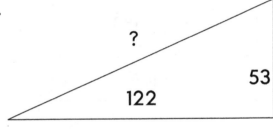

17.

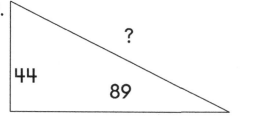

18.

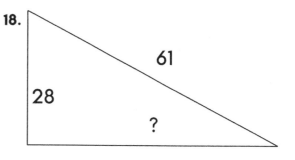

19.

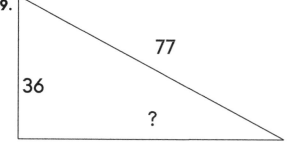

20.

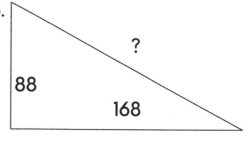

Anna School Learning

21.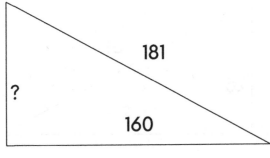

181

?

160

22.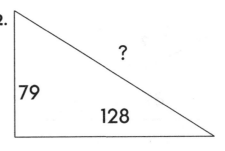

?

79

128

23.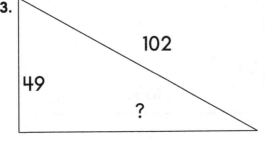

102

49

?

24.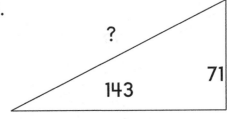

?

143

71

ANSWERS

Page 1:   Order of Operations (PEMDAS)

1. 320	**2.** 64	**3.** 72	**4.** 32	**5.** 16	**6.** 221	**7.** 15
8. 121	**9.** 24	**10.** 72	**11.** 84	**12.** 64	**13.** 7	**14.** 43
15. 27	**16.** 62	**17.** -10	**18.** 63	**19.** 4	**20.** 29	**21.** 794
22. 15	**23.** 26	**24.** 100	**25.** 144	**26.** 196	**27.** 180	**28.** 233
29. 102	**30.** 108	**31.** 16	**32.** 153	**33.** 369	**34.** 40	**35.** 24
36. 0.4	**37.** 15	**38.** 34	**39.** 40	**40.** 2,501	**41.** 7	**42.** 48
43. 52	**44.** 24	**45.** 1	**46.** 22	**47.** 100	**48.** 1,610	**49.** 18
50. 90						

Page 6:   One-Step Equations

1. 3	**2.** 8	**3.** 5	**4.** 10	**5.** 8	**6.** 1
7. 8	**8.** 5	**9.** 9	**10.** 9	**11.** 7	**12.** 8
13. 6	**14.** 9	**15.** 1	**16.** 6 or -1	**17.** 10 or -4	**18.** 3
19. 1	**20.** 9 or -2	**21.** 9 or 0	**22.** 8	**23.** 9	**24.** 4
25. 4	**26.** 1	**27.** 8	**28.** 5	**29.** 3	**30.** 9 or 1
31. 8	**32.** 1	**33.** 6	**34.** 1	**35.** 8	**36.** 3
37. 6	**38.** 5	**39.** 9	**40.** 9	**41.** 4	**42.** 8
43. 1	**44.** 6	**45.** 9	**46.** 7	**47.** 1	**48.** 1
49. 8	**50.** 6				

Page 11:   Two-Step Equations

1. 1	**2.** 2 or -2	**3.** 6	**4.** 5	**5.** 9	**6.** 1
7. 2	**8.** 1 or -1	**9.** 2	**10.** 3	**11.** 4	**12.** 1
13. 4 or -4	**14.** 7	**15.** 3	**16.** 1	**17.** 7	**18.** 1
19. 4 or -5	**20.** 7	**21.** 5	**22.** 2	**23.** 9	**24.** 5
25. 5 or -12	**26.** 5	**27.** 8	**28.** 1	**29.** 7 or -16	**30.** 8 or -8

Page 14:   Multi-Step Equations

1. 1	**2.** 5	**3.** 7 or -13	**4.** 9	**5.** 1	**6.** 2
7. 9 or -9	**8.** 1	**9.** 1 or 14	**10.** 3 or 2	**11.** 2	**12.** 5 or -5

13. 4   **14.** 5   **15.** 2   **16.** 6   **17.** 4   **18.** 1

19. 1   **20.** 3 or –11   **21.** 5   **22.** 9   **23.** 9 or –6   **24.** 3

Page 17: Equations: (One Side)

1. $k = 1$ **2.** $x = 8$ **3.** $z = -10$ **4.** $x = 5$ **5.** $k = -6$ **6.** $z = 18$

7. $x = 3$ **8.** $y = 6$ **9.** $k = -9$ **10.** $m = -5$ **11.** $x = -9$ **12.** $k = -6$

13. $z = 18$ **14.** $z = -2$ **15.** $k = 11$ **16.** $z = 3$ **17.** $x = 12$ **18.** $k = 17$

19. $z = 14$ **20.** $x = 5$ **21.** $y = 4$ **22.** $y = 8$ **23.** $k = 13$ **24.** $y = 17$

25. $y = 4$ **26.** $y = 4$ **27.** $k = -8$ **28.** $k = 18$ **29.** $x = 2$ **30.** $x = 9$

31. $m = -3$ **32.** $x = -9$ **33.** $z = 19$ **34.** $y = 17$ **35.** $m = 20$ **36.** $k = 20$

37. $k = 16$ **38.** $k = 56$ **39.** $y = -1$ **40.** $y = 2$ **41.** $m = 10$ **42.** $k = 8$

43. $z = 12$ **44.** $x = 20$ **45.** $x = -32$ **46.** $y = 2$ **47.** $k = 84$ **48.** $m = 228$

49. $m = -5$ **50.** $k = -8$ **51.** $k = -5$ **52.** $m = -5$ **53.** $m = 10$ **54.** $y = 19$

55. $y = -1$ **56.** $x = -5$ **57.** $y = -3$ **58.** $k = 20$ **59.** $z = 9$ **60.** $z = 0$

Page 23: Equations (Two Sides)

1. $x = 3$ **2.** $y = 7$ **3.** $y = -9$ **4.** $b = -3$ **5.** $b = 5$ **6.** $s = 2$

7. $s = -7$ **8.** $a = 2$ **9.** $z = -8$ **10.** $a = 1$ **11.** $x = -1$ **12.** $x = -6$

13. $a = 1$ **14.** $x = -9$ **15.** $x = 6$ **16.** $a = 2$ **17.** $x = 4$ **18.** $z = -9$

19. $k = 8$ **20.** $b = -2$ **21.** $m = -7$ **22.** $z = 10$ **23.** $z = 6$ **24.** $s = -3$

25. $a = -2$ **26.** $a = 6$ **27.** $y = -10$ **28.** $m = -5$ **29.** $b = -3$ **30.** $x = 2$

31. $k = 5$ **32.** $m = -9$ **33.** $z = 7$ **34.** $b = 3$ **35.** $y = -4$ **36.** $b = 3$

37. $b = -2$ **38.** $y = -6$ **39.** $a = 1$ **40.** $s = 1$ **41.** $x = 10$ **42.** $m = -6$

43. $b = -10$ **44.** $k = -6$ **45.** $b = -6$ **46.** $x = 2$ **47.** $m = 8$ **48.** $m = -10$

49. $k = -4$ **50.** $a = -1$

Page 28: Simplify Expressions

1. $13k + 14$ **2.** $-8k + 11$ **3.** $-3y$ **4.** $8z + 14$ **5.** $7z + 3$

6. $9m$ **7.** $-15y$ **8.** $-6k - 21$ **9.** $-20k$ **10.** $2m - 21$

11. $9x - 8$ **12.** $15k + 1$ **13.** 29 **14.** $20x + 15$ **15.** $-3y - 18$

16. $8x + 3$ **17.** $-25k + 37$ **18.** $24m - 12$ **19.** $108k$ **20.** $-13m$

21. $-14z$ **22.** $16x + 14$ **23.** $4k - 11$ **24.** $-4z - 13$ **25.** $-6k$

26. -k - 25   **27.** 3   **28.** 14x   **29.** 12m   **30.** 4m + 7

31. 6m   **32.** -16x - 7   **33.** 11z   **34.** 13x - 13   **35.** -z - 5

36. 2x + 15   **37.** -9z   **38.** 14k - 24   **39.** -2k + 1   **40.** 17x - 15

41. 4y - 29   **42.** -22y   **43.** -24z - 14   **44.** -11m - 17   **45.** 41y - 8

46. -10x + 10   **47.** -6   **48.** -37m + 14   **49.** -4k + 27   **50.** -3x - 3

51. -6m - 7   **52.** -27x - 16   **53.** 16m + 8   **54.** -10y   **55.** -2z - 1

56. 21y + 1   **57.** 40y + 38   **58.** 13y   **59.** -4x + 2   **60.** -4z

Page 34:   Evaluating Equations

1. -31   **2.** -19   **3.** -189   **4.** 1   **5.** -7   **6.** 8.5   **7.** 82   **8.** -44

Page 35:   Evaluating Equations

1. -217   **2.** -1,624   **3.** 442   **4.** -50   **5.** 478   **6.** 20   **7.** -65

8. 1.6

Page 36:   Evaluating Equations

1. 26   **2.** -7   **3.** -24   **4.** 74   **5.** 0   **6.** 60   **7.** 34   **8.** 6

Page 37:   Evaluating Equations

1. -7   **2.** 7   **3.** -8   **4.** 8   **5.** -10   **6.** -15   **7.** -36   **8.** -3.5

Page 38:   Evaluating Equations

1. -45   **2.** -27   **3.** -23   **4.** 36   **5.** -21   **6.** -168   **7.** -27   **8.** 64

Page 39:   Evaluating Equations

1. -13   **2.** 0   **3.** 7.5   **4.** 16   **5.** -51   **6.** -23   **7.** 70   **8.** 42

Page 40:   Verbal Algebra

1. 6, 48   **2.** 9   **3.** 8   **4.** 9   **5.** 2, 9

6. 8   **7.** 12   **8.** 5, 45   **9.** 10   **10.** 2

11. 5, 2   **12.** 5   **13.** 3, 1   **14.** 10   **15.** 6

16. 4, 40   **17.** 8, 12   **18.** 3, 6   **19.** 8   **20.** 7, 9, 11

21. 0   **22.** 8, 10, 12, 14   **23.** 9   **24.** 14   **25.** 2

26. 3   **27.** 9, 1   **28.** 12, 6   **29.** 6   **30.** 11, 1

Page 45:   Linear Equations

1. 10   **2.** 0   **3.** 6   **4.** 4   **5.** -9   **6.** 9   **7.** 3   **8.** 3   **9.** 9

10. 3   **11.** 4   **12.** 1   **13.** 1   **14.** 1   **15.** 3   **16.** -8   **17.** -8   **18.** 9

19. -2   **20.** 10   **21.** -10   **22.** -10   **23.** 8   **24.** -8   **25.** -8   **26.** -10   **27.** -7

28. -7   **29.** 3   **30.** 8

Page 48: Find Slope from two Points

1. 3   **2.** 0.12   **3.** 5.5   **4.** 0.58   **5.** 1.5   **6.** -0.17   **7.** -1.33

8. 0.11   **9.** -6.2   **10.** -9.5   **11.** 1.12   **12.** 0.8   **13.** -1.27   **14.** -2.33

15. -4.2   **16.** 0.59   **17.** -0.53   **18.** 0.5   **19.** 0.1   **20.** 8.5

Page 50:   Graphing Linear Equations

1. $y = \frac{-3}{2}x + 3$

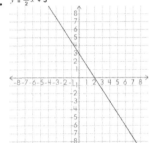

2. $y = \frac{-3}{4}x - 7$

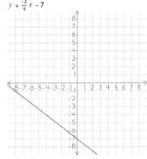

3. $y = -3x - 6$

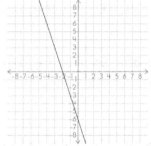

4. $y = \frac{3}{4}x - 5$

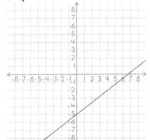

5. $y = 3x$

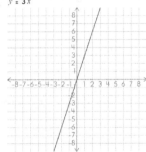

Page 55: Quadratic Equations

1. (1.216, -2.466)
2. (1.106, -1.106)
3. No real solution.
4. (8, -6.5)
5. (-0.531, 7.531)
6. (4.5, -4)
7. (-1.936, 1.136)
8. (0.847, -1.18)

9. (-0.839, 2.553)
10. No real solution.
11. (-3, 4.2)
12. (-1, -3)
13. (2, -2)
14. (5.5, -5.5)
15. (9.568, -1.568)
16. (-8.5, 7)

17. (-1.713, 6.713)
18. (-8.5, 3)
19. (1.091, -0.841)
20. (4.794, -2.294)
21. (-5.333, 4)
22. (1.378, -2.178)
23. (0.6, -2)
24. (-2, -6)

Page 59:   Pythagorean Theorem

1. S=101.573   **2.** S=52.962   **3.** S=183.412   **4.** S=43.589   **5.** S=36.180

6. S=103.730   **7.** S=92.590   **8.** S=194.258   **9.** S=105.071   **10.** S=136.722

11. S=79.145   **12.** S=163.325   **13.** S=208.569   **14.** S=66.970   **15.** S=75.180

16. S=133.015   **17.** S=99.282   **18.** S=54.194   **19.** S=68.066   **20.** S=189.652

21. S=84.623   **22.** S=150.416   **23.** S=89.459   **24.** S=159.656

Anna School Learning

MATH PRE ALGEBRA WORKBOOK

For Beginners

Operations with Integers, Decimals, and Mixed Numbers, Exponents, Roots, Place Value, Percentage, Word Problems, Conversions, and Solving One-Step and One Side Equations

Step by Step Guide

Answer Key Included

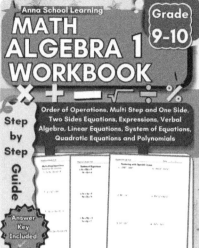

Anna School Learning

MATH ALGEBRA 1 WORKBOOK

Grade 9-10

Order of Operations, Multi Step and One Side, Two Sides Equations, Expressions, Verbal Algebra, Linear Equations, System of Equations, Quadratic Equations and Polynomials

Step by Step Guide

Answer Key Included

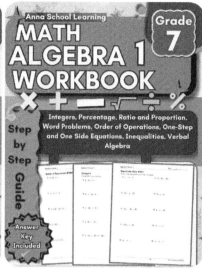

Anna School Learning

MATH ALGEBRA 1 WORKBOOK

Grade 7

Integers, Percentage, Ratio and Proportion, Word Problems, Order of Operations, One-Step and One Side Equations, Inequalities, Verbal Algebra

Step by Step Guide

Answer Key Included

Anna School Learning

MATH ALGEBRA 1 WORKBOOK

Grade 7-9

Integers, Order of Operations, One to Multi Step and Two Sides Equations, Expressions, Verbal Algebra, Inequalities, Linear Equations, System of Equations, Quadratic Equations and Polynomials

Step by Step Guide

Answer Key Included

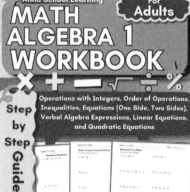

Anna School Learning

MATH ALGEBRA 1 WORKBOOK

For Adults

Operations with Integers, Order of Operations, Inequalities, Equations (One Side, Two Sides), Verbal Algebra Expressions, Linear Equations, and Quadratic Equations

Step by Step Guide

Answer Key Included

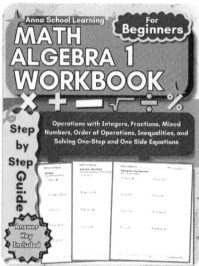

Anna School Learning

MATH ALGEBRA 1 WORKBOOK

For Beginners

Operations with Integers, Fractions, Mixed Numbers, Order of Operations, Inequalities, and Solving One-Step and One Side Equations

Step by Step Guide

Answer Key Included

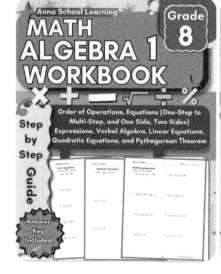

Anna School Learning

MATH ALGEBRA 1 WORKBOOK

Grade 8

Order of Operations, Equations (One-Step to Multi-Step, and One Side, Two Sides) Expressions, Verbal Algebra, Linear Equations, Quadratic Equations, and Pythagorean Theorem

Step by Step Guide

Answer Key Included

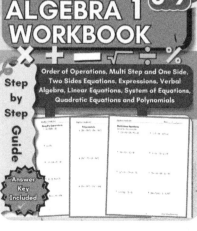

Anna School Learning

MATH ALGEBRA 1 WORKBOOK

Grade 8-9

Order of Operations, Multi Step and One Side, Two Sides Equations, Expressions, Verbal Algebra, Linear Equations, System of Equations, Quadratic Equations and Polynomials

Step by Step Guide

Answer Key Included

Anna School Learning

MATH ALGEBRA 1 WORKBOOK

Grade 9

Equations Multi-Step and two Sides, Expressions, Verbal Algebra, Linear Equations, System of Equations, Quadratic Equations, and Polynomials

Step by Step Guide

Answer Key Included